# WATER
# SCIENCE FAIR
# PROJECTS

JORDAN MCGILL

www.av2books.com

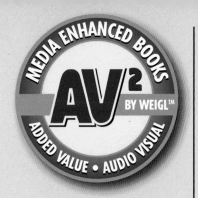

AV[2] provides enriched content that supplements and complements this book. Weigl's AV[2] books strive to create inspired learning and engage young minds in a total learning experience.

## Your AV[2] Media Enhanced books come alive with...

**Audio**
Listen to sections of the book read aloud.

**Key Words**
Study vocabulary, and complete a matching word activity.

**Video**
Watch informative video clips.

**Quizzes**
Test your knowledge.

**Embedded Weblinks**
Gain additional information for research.

**Slide Show**
View images and captions, and prepare a presentation.

Go to **www.av2books.com**, and enter this book's unique code.

## BOOK CODE

### B 52478

AV[2] **by Weigl** brings you media enhanced books that support active learning.

**Try This!**
Complete activities and hands-on experiments.

**... and much, much more!**

---

Published by AV[2] by Weigl Publishers Inc.
350 5th Avenue, 59th Floor
New York, NY 10118
Website: www.av2books.com      www.weigl.com

Library of Congress Cataloging-in-Publication Data

McGill, Jordan.
  Water science fair projects / Jordan McGill.
    p. cm. -- (Science fair projects)
  Includes index.
  ISBN 978-1-61690-652-8 (hardcover : alk. paper) -- ISBN 978-1-61690-656-6 (softcover : alk. paper) -- ISBN 978-1-61690-332-9 (online)
  1. Water--Experiments--Juvenile literature. 2. Science--Methodology--Juvenile literature. 3. Science projects--Juvenile literature. 4. Science fairs--Juvenile literature. I. Title.
  QC920.M34 2012
  551.46078--dc22
                        2011014132

Project Coordinator Jordan McGill
Art Director Terry Paulhus

Printed in North Mankato, Minnesota, in the United States of America
2 3 4 5 6 7 8 9 0 15 14 13 12 11

092011
WEP230911

Every reasonable effort has been made to trace ownership and to obtain permission to reprint copyright material. The publishers would be pleased to have any errors or omissions brought to their attention so that they may be corrected in subsequent printings.

Weigl acknowledges Getty Images as its primary image supplier for this title.

# CONTENTS

8

10

14

18

3

# Take Part in a Science Fair

## WHAT IS A SCIENCE FAIR?

A science fair is an event where students use the **scientific method** to create projects. These projects are then presented to spectators. Judges examine each project and award prizes for following the scientific method and preparing detailed displays. Some science fair winners move on to compete at larger fairs.

## WHY SHOULD YOU TAKE PART IN A SCIENCE FAIR?

Science fairs are an excellent way to learn about topics that interest you. Winning is not the only reason to compete at a science fair. Science fairs are an opportunity for you to work hard on a project and show it off. You will also get to see the projects other students are presenting and learn from them as well.

## ANYTHING ELSE I SHOULD KNOW?

Before you start, you should begin a logbook. A logbook is a handwritten diary of the tasks you performed to complete your science fair project. Include any problems or interesting events that occur.

## WHERE DO I FIND A SCIENCE FAIR?

There are many fairs around the country and worldwide. Ask your teacher if he or she knows if any science fairs are held in your city. Once you find a fair to compete in, you can start preparing your project.

# Eight Steps to a Great Science Fair Project

## STEP 1
### Select a topic

To begin, you must select a topic. Choose a topic that you would like to learn about. That way, working on the project will be exciting.

## STEP 2
### Form a question about your topic

Think of a question you have about your topic. You can ask, "How do clouds form?" Another question could be, "How do glaciers move?"

## STEP 3
### Research your question

Visit a library, and go online to research your topic. Keep track of where you found your **sources** and who wrote them. Most of your time should be spent learning about your topic.

## STEP 4
### Think about the answer to your question

Form a **hypothesis** that may answer your question. The sentence "A cloud forms when water evaporates into the sky and **condenses** onto dust particles" is a hypothesis.

## STEP 5
### Plan an experiment to test your hypothesis

Design an **experiment** that you can repeat and that has observable **reactions**. Make a detailed plan of what you will do in your experiment and what materials you will need. Also include what you will be looking for when you do your experiment.

## STEP 6
### Conduct your experiment and record data

Carry out your experiment, and carefully observe what happens. Take notes. Record data if you need to. If you have nothing to note or record, reconsider whether your experiment has observable reactions.

## STEP 7
### Draw conclusions from your data

Were your predictions right? Sometimes, your hypothesis will be proven wrong. That is fine. The goal is to find the truth, not to be correct. When wrong, scientists think of a new hypothesis and try again.

## STEP 8
### Prepare a report and display

Write a report that explains your project. Include the topic, question, materials, plan, predictions, data, and conclusion in your report. Create a display that you can show at the science fair.

# Picking a Water Science Topic

Water science is the study of water on Earth. All living things on Earth need water to live, so even a small problem in the **water cycle** can have serious effects. Scientists who study water play a key role in understanding the world and keeping it healthy.

This book offers sample experiments for each of the six earth science topics listed below. These experiments can be used to develop a science fair project. Select a topic that interests you. Then, use the sample experiment in this book for your project. You can also think of your own experiment that fits the topic.

## TOPIC 1 GLACIERS

Glaciers are massive blocks of ice that move slowly across Earth. Scientists examine glaciers to learn about Earth's current climate and its climate in the past.

## TOPIC 2 OCEANS, LAKES, AND RIVERS

More than 70 percent of Earth is covered in water. Water environments contain 99 percent of the livable space on the planet. **Oceanographers** who study the depths of the ocean use science and mathematics to explain the interactions between water, **polar ice caps**, the atmosphere, and the **biosphere.**

## TOPIC 3
## PRECIPITATION

Precipitation is rain, snow, hail, and other forms of water that exist in the air. Scientists study precipitation to learn how to predict and influence weather.

## TOPIC 4 THE WATER CYCLE

Water moves from below the ground into the sky and back again in a process called the water cycle. This constant cycle supplies life on Earth with the fresh water it needs to survive. Scientists study the water cycle to learn how even a small change in the water cycle can have large effects.

## TOPIC 5 WATER POLLUTION

Scientists investigate water **pollution** to learn about the damage it causes to the environment. They can then caution people about the dangers of polluting.

## TOPIC 6 WATER POWER

Water has been used for centuries to power machines. It now creates about 10 percent of electricity in the United States. Researchers study water power to find more effective ways to use this **renewable energy** source.

# How Do Glaciers Creep?

## Background Information

Certain conditions need to be in place before a glacier can form. Glaciers only form in areas where it is so cold that the snow does not melt. Snow falls in very cold, moist air. It is light and full of air when it first falls. As more snow falls, it begins to pack. Over time, the air in the bottom layers disappears. The snow becomes ice. Thick layers of ice build up. The ice becomes a glacier. **Gravity** and the ice's weight cause it to move, or flow.

Glacial ice covers about 10 percent of the land on Earth's surface. Glaciers currently cover 5.8 million square miles (15 million square kilometers) of Earth. Most glaciers formed more than 5,000 years ago, but the ice that makes up a glacier is continually renewed. In Alaska, most glacial ice is less than 100 years old, even though the glacier itself is much older.

# EXPERIMENT

One way that glaciers move is called creeping. As snow falls, more **mass** is added to the top of the glacier. This layer becomes so heavy that it flattens deeper layers of snow into packed ice. The solid layers of ice slide over each other and push outward. With each snowfall, more weight is added to the glacier, and it creeps farther outward. Glaciers can creep one direction or in all directions. Perform this experiment to model glacier creep for yourself.

**TIP #1**
Place the model on a slight incline, or create scenery to make the model more accurate.

**TIP #2**
The last step of this experiment helps illustrate how glaciers can carry small rocks as they travel. Over time, the rocks move outside of the glacier and build up into piles called moraines.

## Make a Glacier in 6 Steps

### CAUTION

Messy

### DIFFICULTY

EASY — MEDIUM — HARD

**TIME** 30 minutes

### MATERIALS
- One large bowl
- One cup (250 milliliters) of water
- One large spoon
- One pound (.45 kilograms) of cornstarch
- Two large pieces of wax paper
- Sand, dirt, or gravel

## INSTRUCTIONS

**STEP 1** Put the cornstarch and water in the bowl, and mix them together. The mixture should stick together, but still be a bit runny.

**STEP 2** Place the piece of wax paper in front of you. Using the spoon, place one large scoop of the cornstarch and water mixture in the middle of the wax paper. This is the first part of your glacier.

**STEP 3** Pour a small amount of the mixture on top of the last dollop. This is new snowfall. Notice how the lower layer spreads out under the weight of the addition.

**STEP 4** Spread a thin half-circle of sand, dirt, or gravel near the model glacier.

**STEP 5** Keep adding spoonfuls of the mixture until the glacier reaches the half-circle of gravel. What happens to the gravel? Continue adding spoonfuls until the glacier almost reaches the edge of the wax paper. This is quite similar to how a real glacier moves and grows.

**STEP 6** Place another piece of wax paper on top of the model. Flip it upside down to see the underside of the glacier and how it interacted with the debris. What happened to the debris?

# Why Do People Float Better in Salt Water?

## Background Information

Earth has five oceans. They are the Indian, the Atlantic, the Arctic, the Pacific, and the Southern Oceans. Together, they cover more than 65 percent of Earth. About 97 percent of the world's water is located in oceans.

Rivers and lakes can be found all over the world. Rivers are bodies of water that flow to lakes, oceans, and other rivers. Lakes are large bodies of standing water. Rivers and lakes are home to many plants and animals that have **adapted** to life in and around water.

# EXPERIMENT

Oceans are known for their salt water. Fresh water, on the other hand, has very little salt. As a result, fresh water weighs less than salt water. The more water weighs, the higher its **density**. Surfaces with high density are better able to carry or hold objects that are less dense. As a result, objects should float better in salt water than in fresh water. Follow the steps below to complete your own experiment with salt water and flotation.

**TIP #1**
A useful way to understand density is to imagine a cup filled 3/4 full with salt. The small objects used in the experiment would rest on top of pure salt very well. Each time you add more salt to the water, the mixture is getting closer to a state of pure salt.

## Experiment with Flotation in 6 Steps

**TIP #2**
You can substitute other small objects for those in the materials list.

## CAUTION

Wet

## DIFFICULTY

EASY  MEDIUM  HARD

**TIME** 30 minutes

## MATERIALS

- Eight plastic cups filled with 3/4 of a cup of tap water each
- Salt
- One teaspoon measuring spoon
- One paperclip
- One egg
- One baby carrot
- One toothpick
- One raw rice kernel
- One pebble
- Towel

## INSTRUCTIONS

**STEP 1** Place all eight plastic cups in front of you. Fill each 3/4 full with water. Leave the first cup as it is. Add one teaspoon of salt to the second cup, two teaspoons of salt to the third, three teaspoons of salt to the fourth, and so on, up to the eighth cup.

**STEP 2** Take one of the small objects, such as the paperclip, and add it to the first cup of water. Time how long it takes for the paper clip to drop to the bottom of the cup.

**STEP 3** Take the object out, and dry it with the towel.

**STEP 4** Place the same object in the second cup. Time how long it takes for it to sink. Continue these steps in each cup until the object floats. If it does not float, record that observation.

**STEP 5** Repeat steps 2 to 4 with all the small objects you collected.

**STEP 6** Be sure to take accurate notes as you perform this experiment. To present your findings, make a table that lists the different objects, how long it took for them to reach the bottom of each cup, and which cup contained enough salt to make the object float.

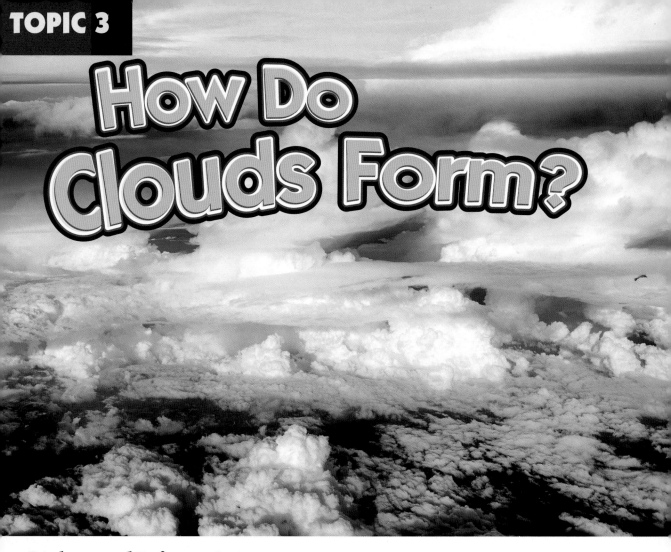

# How Do Clouds Form?

## Background Information

The atmosphere is a blanket of gases that surrounds Earth. One of the gases in the atmosphere is water **vapor**. This gas rises from oceans, lakes, and other bodies of water when the Sun warms them. Water vapor cools as it rises. Then, it condenses and forms tiny drops of water. When the drops become large enough, they fall as rain or snow.

Water that falls to Earth is called **precipitation**. At all times, the atmosphere contains enough water for 1 inch (2.5 cm) of rain to fall on Earth.

Precipitation is an important part of the water cycle. It redistributes water around the world and allows plants and animals to get the water they need to survive.

# EXPERIMENT

**TIP #1**
The black paper is not essential to the success of the experiment. It will, however, help you see the cloud.

For a cloud to form, three conditions must be met. First, there must be water vapor in the air. Second, the air must decrease in temperature. Third, there must be small particles floating in the air on which the water can gather and condense. In this experiment, you will create the conditions needed to create a cloud.

**TIP #2**
Be sure to document and explain why each step is important in your report.

## Form a Cloud in 7 Steps

### CAUTION

Fire    Adult's Help    Sticky

### DIFFICULTY

EASY    MEDIUM    HARD

**TIME** 30 minutes

### MATERIALS
- One clear 2-liter pop bottle
- One 2-liter bottle lid
- One sheet of black paper
- Matches
- Water

## INSTRUCTIONS

**STEP 1** Remove the label from the plastic bottle.

**STEP 2** Fill the bottom of the bottle with about 2 inches (5 centimeters) of water. Blow into the bottle so that it is not crushed anywhere. Then, seal the bottle.

**STEP 3** For at least one minute, shake the bottle hard. This releases water vapors into the air.

**STEP 4** With an adult's help, light a match. Open the bottle quickly and drop the match inside. Then, quickly screw the cap back on. The match will create steam when it hits the water.

**STEP 5** Lay the black paper on a table in front of you. Lay the bottle sideways on top of the paper.

**STEP 6** Press as hard as you can on the bottle. Observe. If no cloud forms, press on the bottle again for 10 seconds. Observe again. Continue to do so until a cloud forms. By pressing on the bottle, you are increasing the air pressure inside the bottle.

**STEP 7** Once a cloud appears, quickly unscrew the bottle, and watch it float away.

# What are the Different Forms of Water?

## Background Information

Water is found in oceans, rivers, ponds, and puddles. Water is also found in air. Every day, water rises into the sky. It also returns to the ground. This process is called the water cycle. Sunshine, air, water, and the force of gravity work together as part of the water cycle.

Most of Earth's water is liquid, but water can also be a gas or a solid. Every day, the Sun heats 1 trillion tons (907 billion tonnes) of water in oceans and on land. This heated water becomes water vapor. Water vapor may be invisible. It may also appear as fog, clouds, or steam.

Ice, snow, hail, and frost are water in its solid form. About two percent of Earth's water is found in icecaps, glaciers, and other forms of ice and snow.

# EXPERIMENT

By subjecting water to hotter and colder temperatures, you can change its form. In this experiment, you explore the possible states of water.

**TIP #1**
Water becomes a gas when the temperature reaches 212° Fahrenheit (100° Celsius). It becomes a solid at 32° Fahrenheit (0° C).

## Examine Water's Forms in 6 Steps

**TIP #2**
Try turning a solid into a liquid and a gas into a liquid to reverse the transformations in this experiment.

## INSTRUCTIONS

**CAUTION**

Fire    Adult's Help

**DIFFICULTY**

EASY    MEDIUM    HARD

**TIME** 50 minutes

**MATERIALS**
- Water
- Pot
- Two clear plastic cups
- Flashlight

**STEP 1** Fill a clear cup with water. Note how the water moves, how it is contained by the cup, and how easily you can see through the water. Record your observations on water in its liquid form in a notebook or on a piece of paper.

**STEP 2** Fill the other cup with water, and pour it into the pot. Then, fill the cup with water again, and place it in the freezer.

**STEP 3** With an adult's help, place the pot on the stove. Bring the water to a boil. You should be able to see gas rising from the pot.

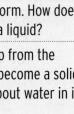

**STEP 4** Record your observations about water in its gas form. How does it differ from water as a liquid?

**STEP 5** Remove the cup from the freezer. The water has become a solid. Record observations about water in its solid form.

**STEP 6** Use your notes to make a table comparing the different properties of water in each of its forms.

# How Can an Oil Spill be Cleaned?

## Background Information

Water **recycles** itself through the water cycle. When pollution enters water, it spreads through the water cycle. Pollution that enters in one stage of the water cycle can have serious negative effects further along in the cycle.

Most water pollution comes from businesses, farms, and sewage. Sometimes, this waste is dumped directly into water supplies. However, water supplies can become polluted indirectly as well. **Emissions** from cars and factories can be found in rainwater. Rainwater then travels from the ground into water sources, such as lakes and rivers. To protect water supplies, pollution must be prevented at all stages of the water cycle.

# EXPERIMENT

In this experiment, you will model an oil spill and try to clean it up. Oil spills float in the water and pollute all things that live there. The water becomes undrinkable, and animals and plants often become coated in thick, black oil. Cleanup crews must act quickly to save the environment. To clean the water, large boats are used to skim the oil from the water. **Sorbents** are used to absorb the oil. Using your model of an oil spill, find out what substances act as the best sorbents.

**TIP #1**
Add more oil if the tray is larger than 1 square foot (30 square centimeters).

**TIP #2**
Try to think of other materials that might clean up an oil spill.

## Clean an Oil Spill in 7 Steps

### CAUTION

Messy    Wet    Sticky

### DIFFICULTY

EASY   MEDIUM   HARD

**TIME** 40 minutes

### MATERIALS

- Water
- Cup
- A large, deep tray or bowl
- Three tablespoons of cooking oil
- Two tablespoons of cocoa powder
- A Spoon
- Cotton ball, grass, paper towels, a sponge, and a styrofoam cup
- Hair
- A feather
- A green leaf
- Dish detergent

## INSTRUCTIONS

**STEP 1** Fill the tray 1/2 full with water.

**STEP 2** Pour the cooking oil into the cup. Add the cocoa powder. Mix the cocoa powder and oil together. This represents oil.

**STEP 3** Dump the oil mixture into the water. Then, watch the oil spread.

**STEP 4** Try to skim the oil from the surface of the water with the spoon. How much oil do you recover?

**STEP 5** Use the other materials to discover which absorbs the oil spill best. Be sure to make detailed notes about each material and its interaction with the oil. Which material worked best? Why was this material more effective than the others?

**STEP 6** Dip the hair and feather into the oily water. Record how the oil affects the hair, feather, and leaf.

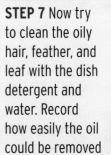

**STEP 7** Now try to clean the oily hair, feather, and leaf with the dish detergent and water. Record how easily the oil could be removed from these objects. Think about the permanent effects an oil spill can have on the environment.

# How Can Water Power Machines?

## Background Information

Electricity makes machines run. Coal, gas, and oil are often used to create electricity. These energy sources are called fossil fuels. Fossil fuels are a non-renewable resource. This means they will run out over time.

Water can also be used to create electricity. Water power is a renewable source of energy. This is because water constantly recycles itself through the water cycle.

The movement of water is powerful and creates energy. Special machines change this energy into electricity. Electricity that comes from water power is called hydroelectricity.

The energy created by water falling from a high level to a low level can be used to create electricity. Large waterfalls, such as Niagara Falls, create electricity in this way. Falling water is directed into long pipes connected to a power station. The force of the moving water makes waterwheels spin inside the power station. The spinning waterwheels cause machines called turbines to turn. These turbines create electricity.

# EXPERIMENT

In this experiment, you will create your own water wheel. The force of moving water will be transferred and used to lift a weight. This experiment will show you how water power is harnessed and used. Modern hydroelectricity is made in much the same way, but with the additional step of turbines converting the mechanical energy to electrical energy.

**TIP #1**
The water wheel can be more effective if more paddles are added. The more paddles you add, the less energy is wasted.

**TIP #2**
The stick should be able to spin in the bucket freely without the glued pieces hitting the sides.

## Make a Water Wheel in 6 Steps

### CAUTION

Messy    Wet    Adult's Help

### DIFFICULTY

EASY    MEDIUM    HARD

**TIME** 60 minutes

### NECESSARY MATERIALS
- A large bucket
- A long stick or pole
- Two empty yogurt containers
- String
- Milk carton
- Scissors
- White glue
- A small object to use as a weight
- Water

### INSTRUCTIONS

**STEP 1** Make sure that the stick is long enough to span the top of the bucket. With an adult's help, carve a small groove into each side of the bucket so that the stick will stay in place. Place the stick in the grooves.

**STEP 2** Cut two sides off the milk carton so that you have two rectangles. Glue the two rectangles together with the stick stuck between them. They should be glued near the middle of the stick to make a paddle. The stick should turn when you apply pressure to either side of paddle.

**STEP 3** Make sure the stick can spin freely while placed on the bucket. Also, make sure it stays in the cut grooves.

**STEP 4** Tie a small object to one end of the string. Wrap the other end of the string to the stick where it protrudes from the bucket. Glue that end of the string to make sure it stays.

**STEP 5** Fill both yogurt containers with water. Slowly pour the water from the yogurt containers onto one side of the paddle.

**STEP 6** Continue to pour water onto the paddle so that the stick turns and lifts the weighted object. This is a very simple form of machine that is powered by water.

# Preparing Your Report

Once your experiment is completed, write a report. The purpose of the report is to summarize your work. You want others to understand the question, the research, and the experiment. The report also explains your results and ties everything together in a conclusion.

## 1 Title
The title of your report should be the question you are trying to answer.

## 2 Purpose
This section of the report should include a few sentences explaining why you chose this project.

## 3 Hypothesis
The hypothesis is made up of one sentence that explains the answer your experiment was meant to prove.

## 4 Background
Write a summary of the information you found during your research. You most likely will not need to use all of your research.

## 5 Materials
Write a list of the materials you used during your experiment. This is the same as the list of materials included with each sample experiment in this book.

## 6 Plan
Write out the steps needed to carry out your experiment.

## 7 Results
Write all observations and relevant data you recorded during your experiment here. Include any tables or graphs you made.

## 8 Conclusion
In this part of the report, state what you learned. Be sure to write how you think your results prove or disprove your hypothesis. You should also write your hypothesis again somewhere in this section. It is acceptable if your hypothesis was false. What is important is that you were creative and followed the scientific method.

## 9 Bibliography
Include an alphabetical list by the author's last name of all sources you used.

# Making Your Display

Most science fairs encourage the use of a backboard to display your project. Most displays use a three-panel backboard. It stands up on its own and is easy to view.

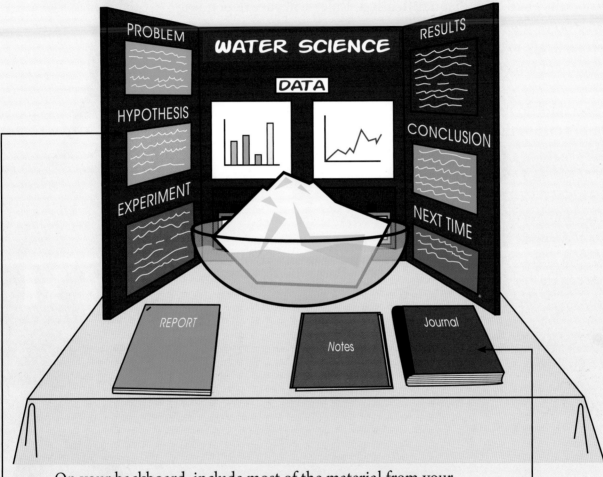

- On your backboard, include most of the material from your report. Leave out the background information. You may also include photos or drawings to help explain your project.

- Most often, your backboard will be placed on a table. On the table, you can include any models you created or samples you collected. Also include the logbook and a copy of your report.

- If possible, you may also perform your experiment at the fair.

# Impressing the Judges

## Know the Rules

Judges expect that you know the rules. Breaking rules can lead to lost points and even **disqualification**. Rules will vary depending on who is organizing the science fair. Before you begin your project, talk to the organizers of the fair you plan to compete in. Ask them for a list of rules.

Most fairs do not allow any dangerous materials, such as flames or organisms that could make someone sick.

## Practice Presenting

To stand out at the science fair, you have to give a strong presentation to the judges. Write a short speech that covers what you want to say. Your speech should summarize why you chose the project. It should also explain the experiment and your conclusions. Practice this speech until you are comfortable. Speak confidently and clearly.

Many judges will ask questions. Present your project to friends and family. Then, have them ask questions as if they were judges.

## Dress For an Event

A science fair is a special event. It is different from an ordinary day. When you go somewhere special, do your parents have you dress up? Judges look at every part of your presentation, including you. Wear something special. Comb your hair. Tuck in your shirt. Tie your shoes. You are presenting yourself as much as your project.

# Glossary

**adapted:** adjusted to make suitable

**biosphere:** the part of Earth and its atmosphere in which living organisms exist or that is capable of supporting life

**condenses:** become denser

**density:** the state of being closely set

**disqualification:** to be eliminated from a competition

**emissions:** substances discharged into the air

**experiment:** a test, trial, or procedure

**gravity:** a force that moves things toward the center of a planet

**hypothesis:** a possible explanation for a scientific question

**mass:** the quantity of matter as determined from its weight

**oceanographer:** a researcher who studies the ocean

**polar ice cap:** sea ice formed from the freezing of sea water as well as glaciers formed from falling snow

**pollution:** contamination of air, water, and soil

**precipitation:** water that falls from the sky

**reactions:** when two or more substances combine to make a new chemical substance

**recycles:** extracts useful materials from

**renewable energy:** energy that is replaced rapidly by natural processes

**scientific method:** a system of observation

**sorbents:** materials that can absorb other materials

**sources:** the books or websites from which research was obtained

**vapor:** water floating in the air

**water cycle:** the cycle by which water moves around Earth

# Log on to www.av2books.com

AV² by Weigl brings you media enhanced books that support active learning. Go to www.av2books.com, and enter the special code found on page 2 of this book. You will gain access to enriched and enhanced content that supplements and complements this book. Content includes video, audio, web links, quizzes, a slide show, and activities.

## Audio
Listen to sections of the book read aloud.

## Video
Watch informative video clips.

## Embedded Weblinks
Gain additional information for research.

## Try This!
Complete activities and hands-on experiments.

---

# WHAT'S ONLINE?

|  Try This! |  Embedded Weblinks |  Video | EXTRA FEATURES |
|---|---|---|---|
| Create useful observation sheets. Make a judging sheet. Make a timeline to make sure projects are finished on time. Complete fun interactive activities. | Check out more information about **water science** topics. Learn how to coordinate a science fair. Learn more about creating an effective display. | Watch a video about water science. Check out another video about **water science**. |  **Audio** Listen to sections of the book read aloud.  **Key Words** Study vocabulary, and complete a matching word activity.  **Slide Show** View images and captions, and prepare a presentation. **Quizzes** Test your knowledge. |

---

**AV² was built to bridge the gap between print and digital. We encourage you to tell us what you like and what you want to see in the future.**

## Sign up to be an AV² Ambassador at www.av2books.com/ambassador.